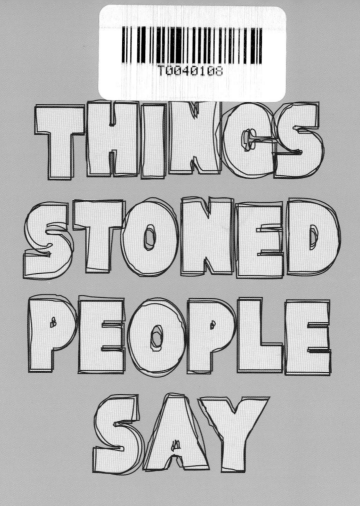

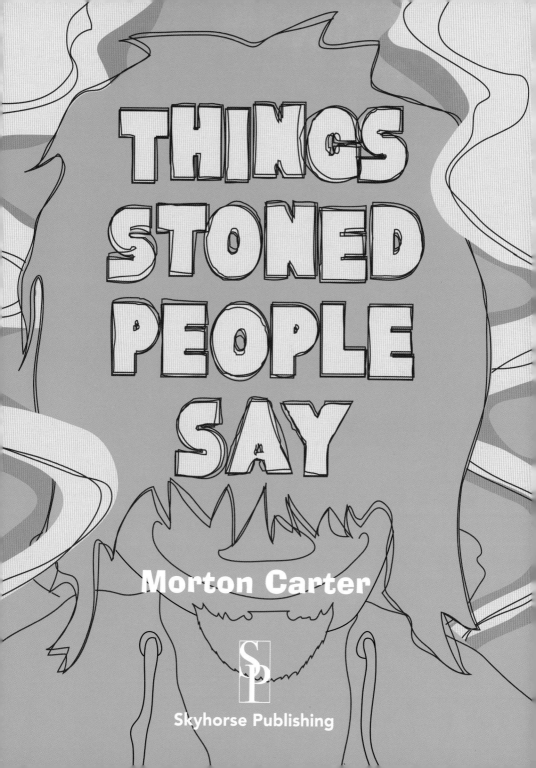

THINGS STONED PEOPLE SAY

Morton Carter

Skyhorse Publishing

Skyhorse Publishing books may be purchased in bulk at special discounts for sales promotion, corporate gifts, fund-raising, or educational purposes. Special editions can also be created to specifications. For details, contact the Special Sales Department, Skyhorse Publishing, 307 West 36th Street, 11th Floor, New York, NY 10018 or info@skyhorsepublishing.com.

Skyhorse® and Skyhorse Publishing® are registered trademarks of Skyhorse Publishing, Inc.®, a Delaware corporation.

Visit our website at www.skyhorsepublishing.com.

10 9 8 7 6 5 4 3 2 1

Library of Congress Cataloging-in-Publication Data is available on file.
ISBN: 978-1-62087-638-1

Printed in India

For you, the reader.

Contents

introduction

When you're a kid, your parents will tell you that life is hard. Later, when you're an adult yourself, you'll take it one step further. You'll learn that most of the time, life sucks. Sitting on your second-hand couch, looking up at your water-stained ceiling, you'll wonder why it all has to be so frigging hard.

Thankfully, though, we have the benefit of history, and the wisdom of philosophers, artists, and great men and women of science to help guide us through these troubled and frustrating moments.

However, I find some of the most brilliant things—the kind that poetically encapsulate the human condition—are spoken by us regular everyday folks on everyday drugs like marijuana.

The stoner in your life is a gift. He is a personal philosopher, ready to give you a good dose of sudden wisdom. Sometimes it might sound like nonsense or inapplicable to your condition or full of spoonerisms, but it is the kind of wisdom we need more of in this accelerated age. The wisdom of the stoner lies not in answers, but in the questions.

In our age, everyone is trying to sell answers. Answers about the latest diet where you only eat seeds, how to kick addictions you didn't know you had, picking a religion that's right for you, and even how to arrange your furniture to increase your income. Answers, answers everywhere and not a drop to drink. That's why we are so messed up in the first place. Everyone thinks they know the real path to happiness, and we're willing to listen to anyone.

A stoner, however, has gained the greatest gift of all, a questioning mind. Socrates—who by all accounts was very wise—said it best: "All I know is that I know nothing." And nobody knows nothing better than a stoner. The weed frees us from the great shackles of society's rules. On drugs, questions such as "Who discovered Christopher Columbus?" or "What are all these lights for?" are not the words of a simpleton, but those of a curious observer.

The more closely we observe the world, the more hilarious it becomes. Why do we do the things we do? We wear ridiculous, glittery clothes to attract mates. We take jobs we hate in industries we ideologically despise because we need money for food and shelter. We watch television shows about people drinking and fighting each other because that's what comes on. We watch movies that we know are terrible, simply to be able to talk about how much we hated watching them. These are all really silly. The stoner, however, laughs at these things. The stoner sees the world as it truly is, pieced together sloppily, with various pieces of tape holding it together.

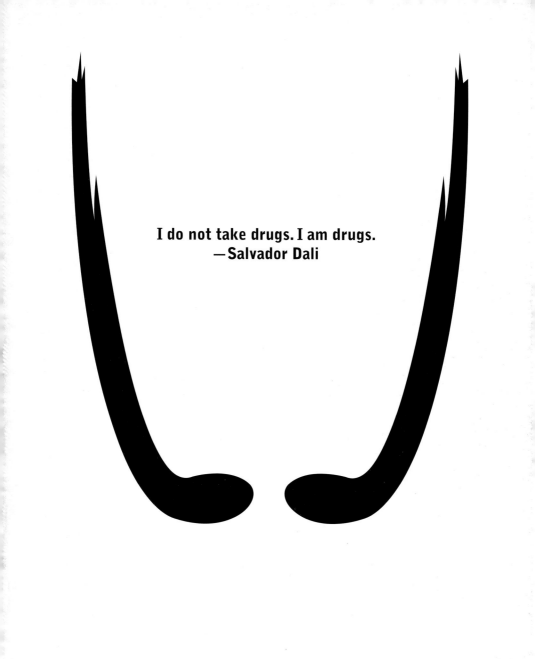

I do not take drugs. I am drugs.
—Salvador Dali

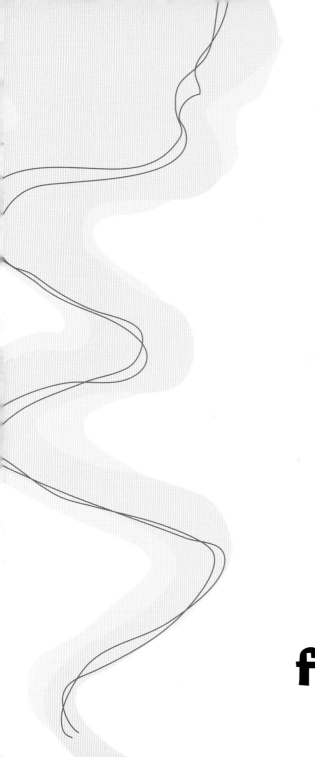

food

We all need to eat to survive, but food is a completely different experience for the stoner. It is an exploration of tastes, smells, textures, and memories. The simplest chocolate chip cookie becomes a roller coaster of sugary crunch and buttery joy, taking us on a ride through happy childhood memories, filling our heart and stomach with pleasure.

Good munchies are the key to a blissed-out experience. Disaster falls when the cookie jar is empty. The last thing you need to do when you are high is go to a supermarket. Too many choices. The packaging on the food looks weird. The lights are too bright. The clerks are all judging you (they know!). Do yourself a favor and plan ahead. It will keep you from crying in the chip aisle.

After all, a stoner gets stoned to have a good time, and you can make a good time better with a nice spread...

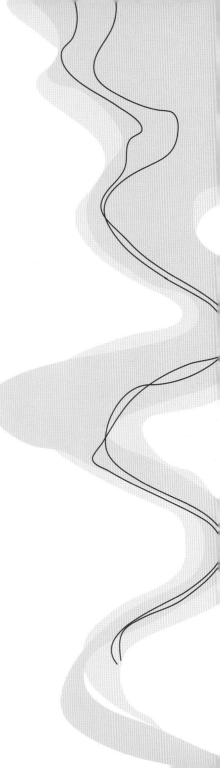

God created
pumpkin bread,

then God created
this pumpkin bread.

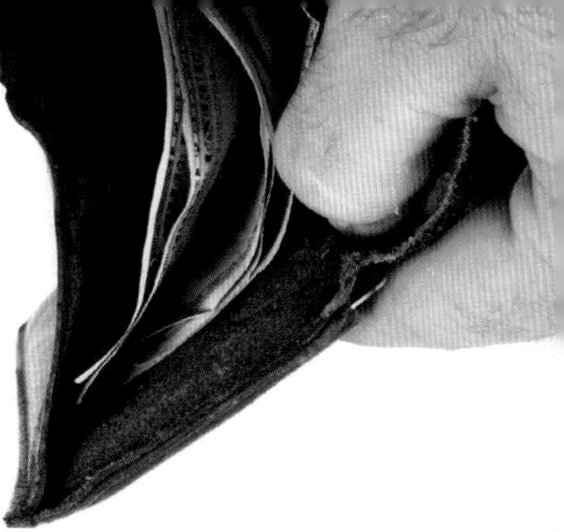

HERE! TURN MY WALLET INTO NACHOS!

USE YOUR MAGIC, WIZARD!

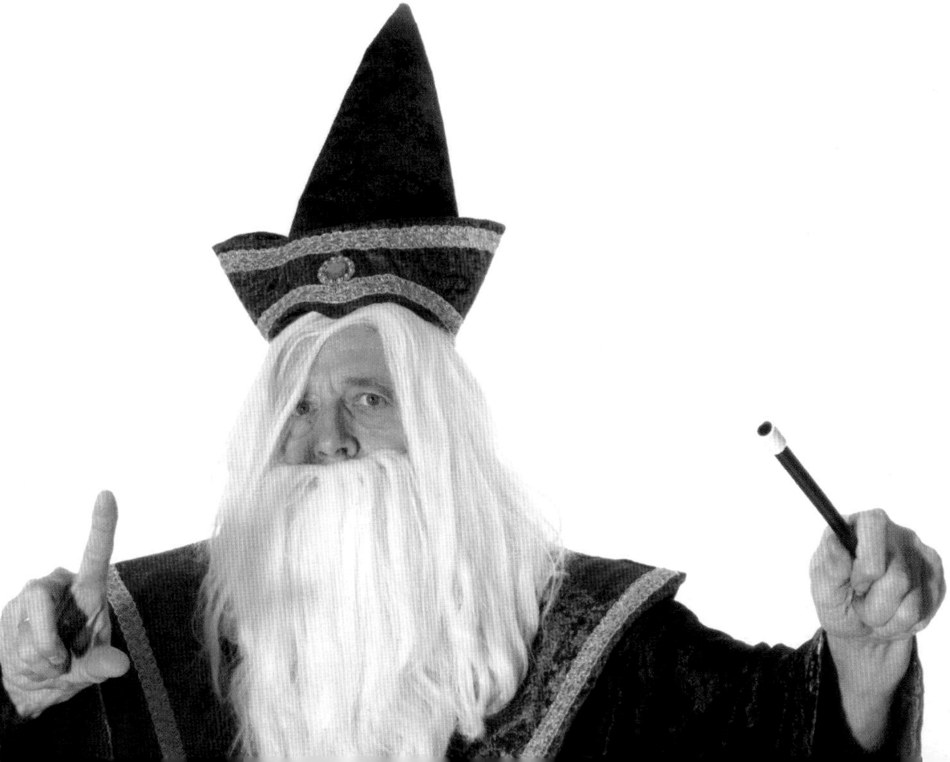

SOMETIMES

I FORGET TO

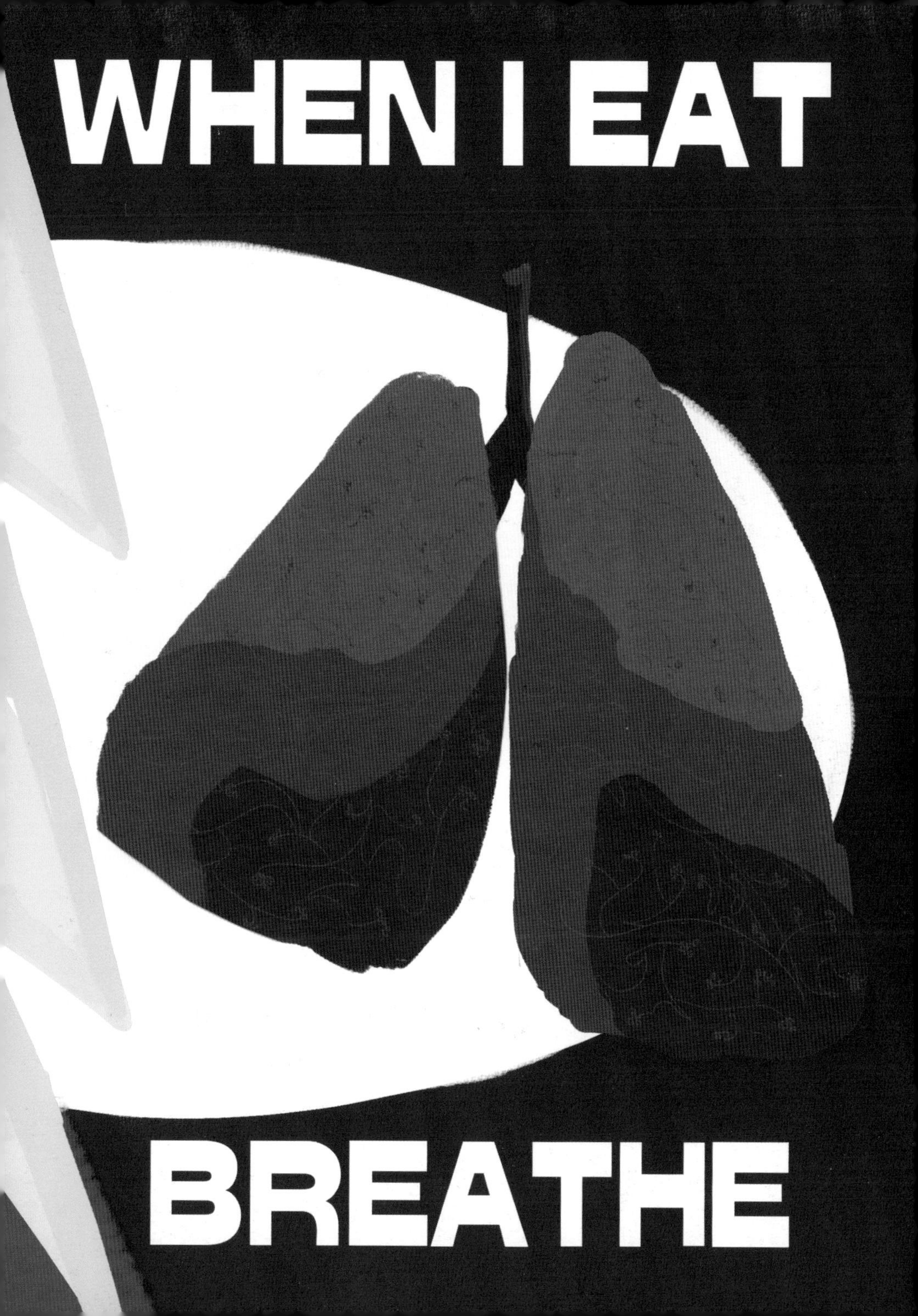
WHEN I EAT
BREATHE

WHAT GLORIOUS THINGS COME FROM A BIRD PUSSY!

"What do you call cheese that's not yours?"

"Nacho cheese?"

"I was gonna call it Stolen Cheese,

or as the British call it:

Thievescheddar."

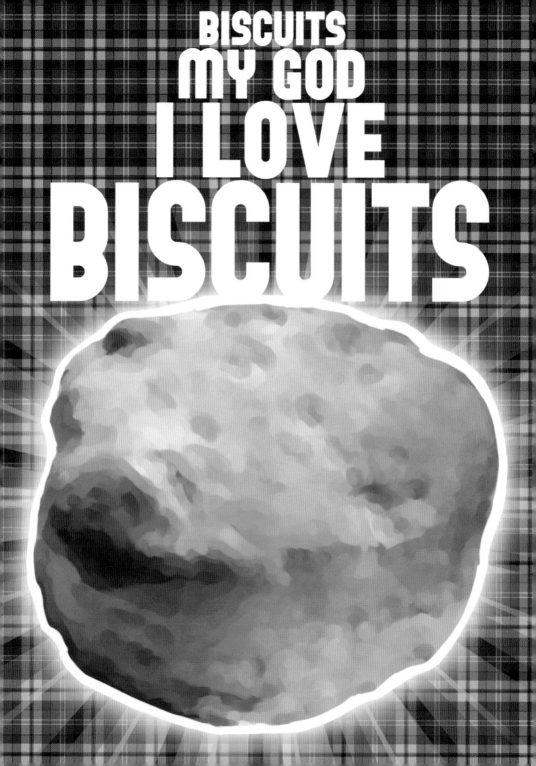

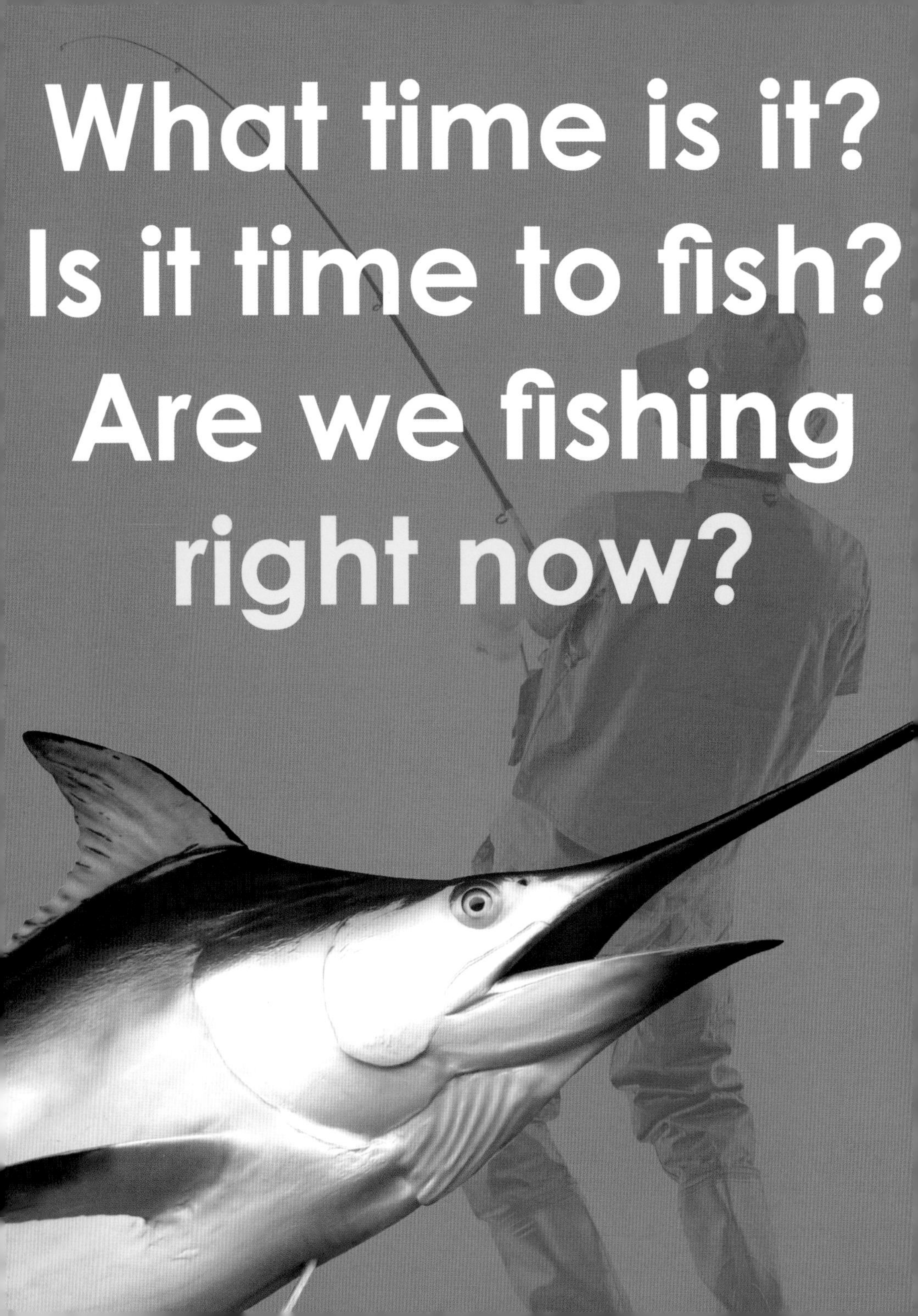
What time is it?
Is it time to fish?
Are we fishing
right now?

YOU HAVE THE BEST PIZZA CRUST EATING STRATEGY!

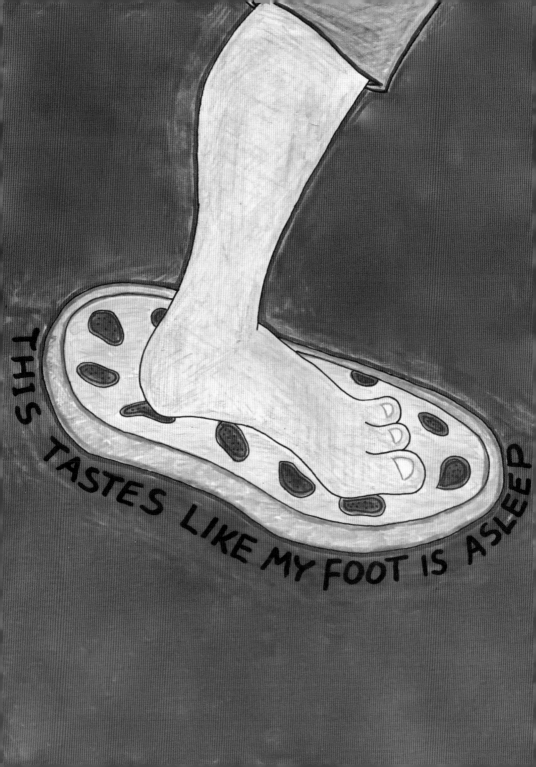

I'D RATHER HAVE THE MUNCHIES THAN A HANGOVER.

I PUT THE FRIDGE IN THE BEER.

now i know why people get high. i sat in the same chair for about three hours and the only thing i worried about was how far away my chinese food was.

I love french fries.
I love everything French.
Are they really French?
Did French kissing come
from France?

That just doesn't make
any sense.

I wish I had a sandwich with my hair in it.

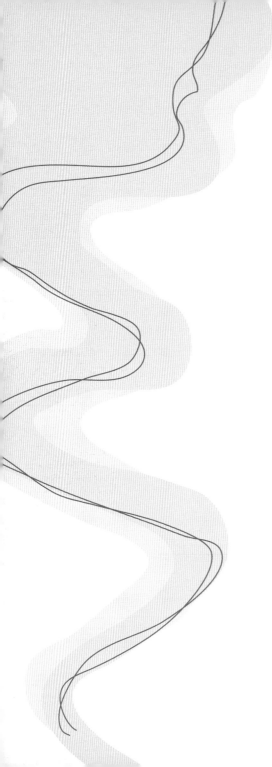

sex

There is something all of our ancestors had in common. It's not eye color or the ability to curl the tip of the tongue. It's not height or weight. The only thing all of your ancestors have in common is that they've all had sex. (Sorry for making you think about your relatives doing it.)

Sex is as human and as normal a thing as anything—maybe even the most human. In our attempts to become more civilized, though, leaders of men have tried to make sex into something weird, gross, and shameful. (Actually, they've tried to do the same thing with our friend, the cannabis plant. Thank god they haven't outlawed sex yet.)

The stoner's wisdom gives us special insight into most things. Sex loses its priority if everything you experience feels just as awesome. But as the focus on getting sex is lessened, the sexual mystery increases. No one plays hard-to-get better than a stoner, mainly because it's hard to get their attention in the first place...

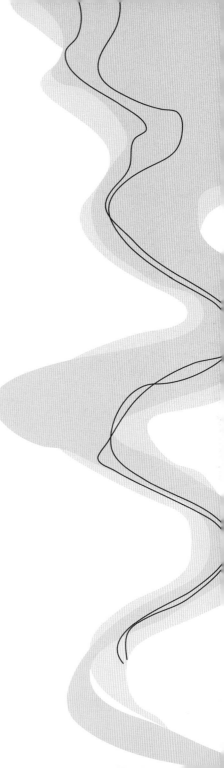

I'VE NEVER THOUGHT OF ERECTIONS LIKE THIS BEFORE.
I'M SO FRIGHTENED OF THEM.

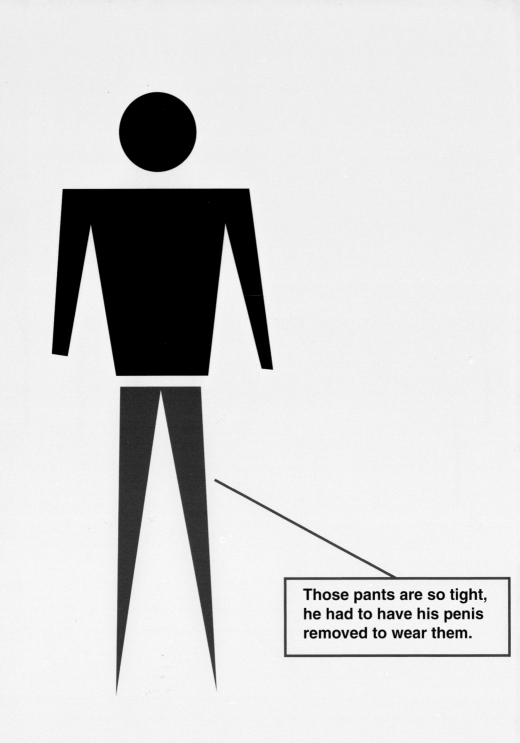

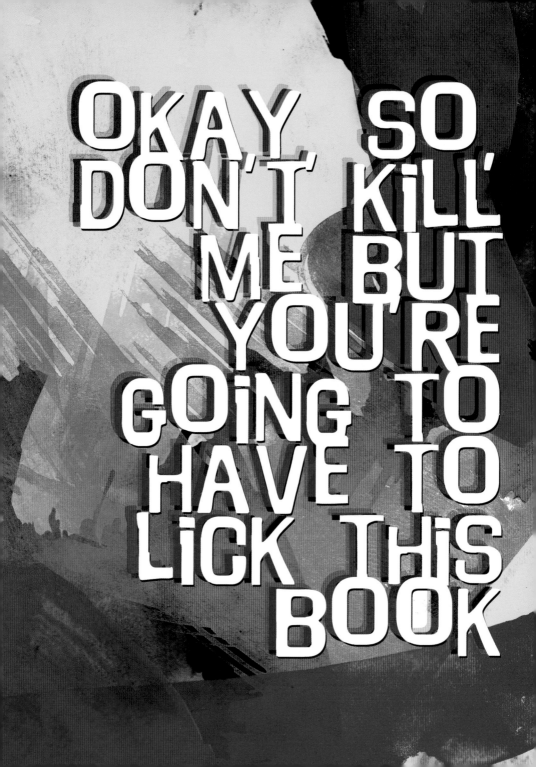

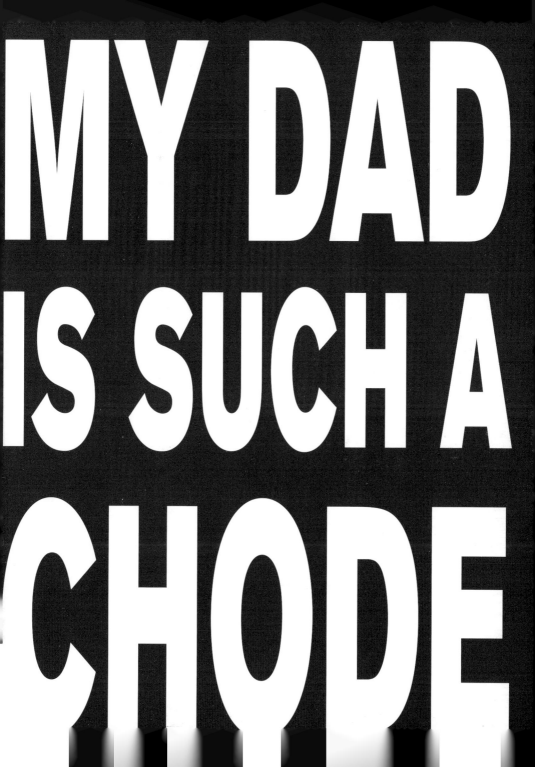

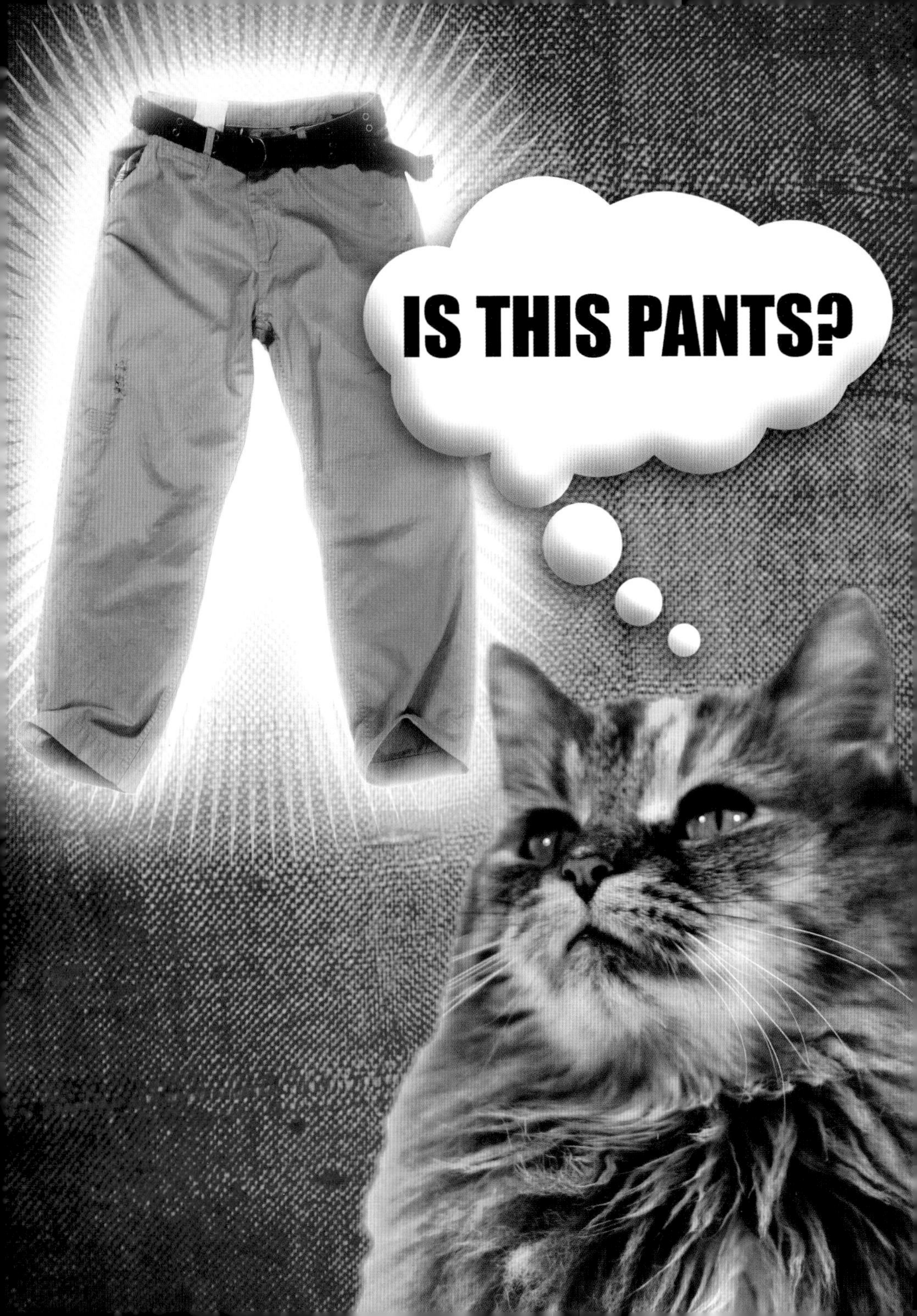
IS THIS PANTS?

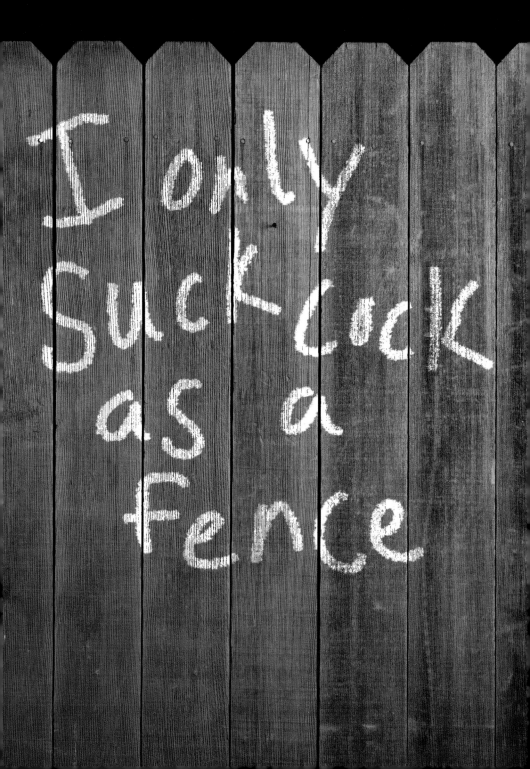

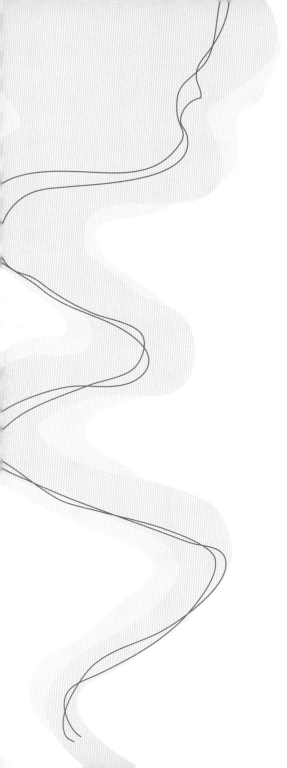

weed

Stoners hold great reverence for their weed. It's the gateway to elevated thinking, elevated feeling, and a better television-watching experience. Weed brings people together: not just stoners, but also the people the stoners talk to at a party.

Weed is forever evolving, so being stoned is never the same experience. You might feel it in your body, your brain, your stomach, or in the air around you—regardless of the CIA-regulated mind-control nanorobots. Whether you are high, hungry, or paranoid, the wisdom of the stoner comes through with clarity (well, sometimes).

So, let us now take in the wisdom of stoners as they contemplate the secrets of the stoned, the mysteries of marijuana, and the "why?" of weed.

Also, we're lucky that they shut up about weed long enough to tell us about anything else…

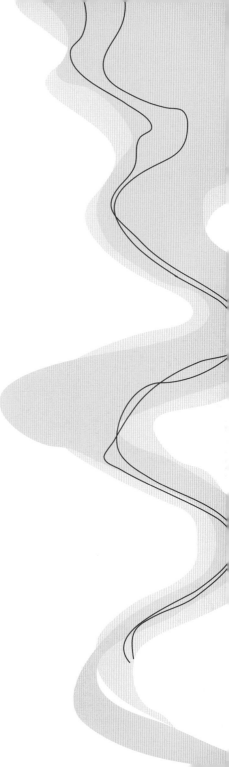

MY BRAIN GETS FRIED
SO MANY FASTERS.

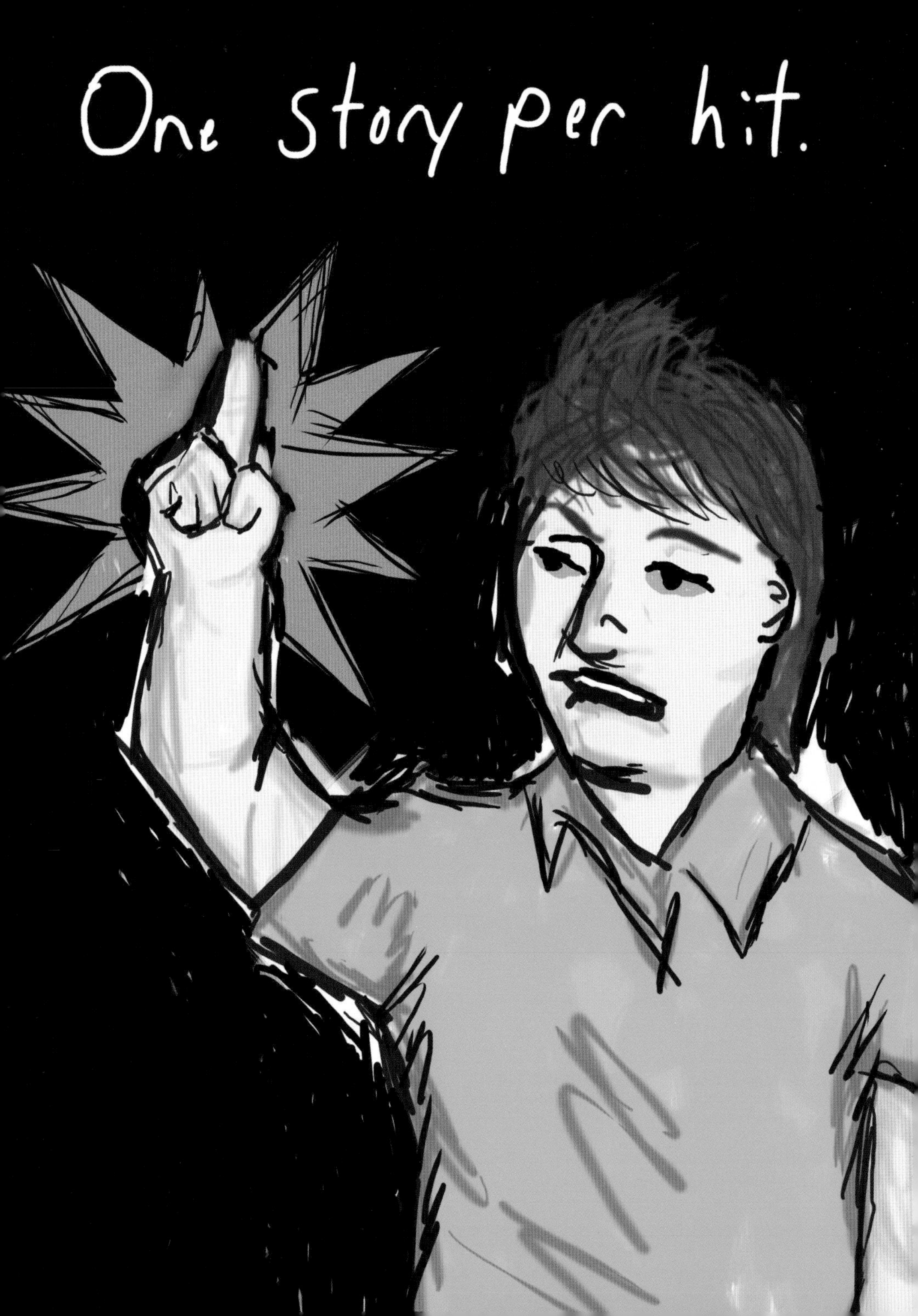
One story per hit.

What if deja vu is
the feeling we get
when we get pulled out
of our own timeline and
get placed back in it,
but a split second too
soon?

"THAT SHADOW IN THE WINDOW IS THE PERFECT SHAPE."
WHAT'S THE PERFECT SHAPE?
"a SMALL, HOODED man."

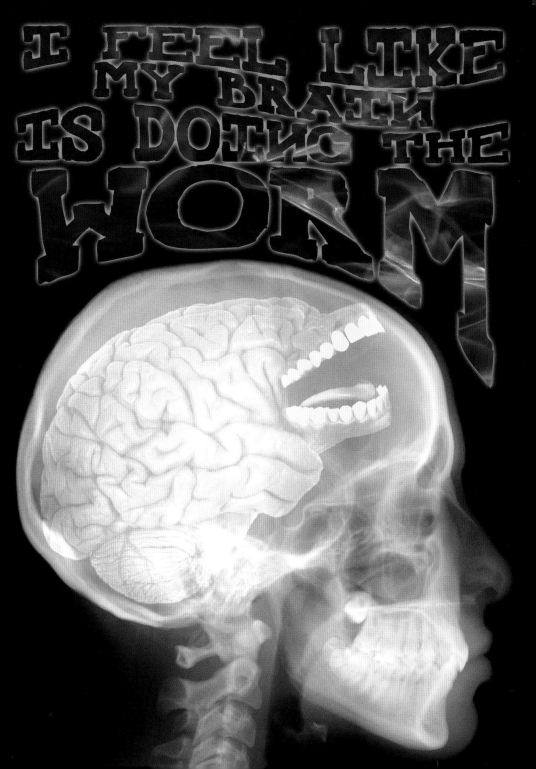

I wonder where the smoke goes after it gets you stoned.

Is smoking pot really bad for you? I mean worse than smoking cigarettes? It seems cleaner to me.

I'm too phoned to stone home.

If by "go out,"
you mean
"sit on the balcony
with a Dutch Master,"
then, yes,
I'm going out tonight.

I wasn't sure if i was a real person anymore, so i had to look in the mirror.

WHOA!
I just realized the lights were on.

That joint is so big, it looks like Sir Walter Raleigh rolled it.

I am wearing my
mountain climbing wetsuit.

I'm so stoned, I wanna run toward the ocean while screaming at it.

I love the beach... except for all the sand.

WHENEVER I GET HIGH ANYMORE, I JUST EAT IT.

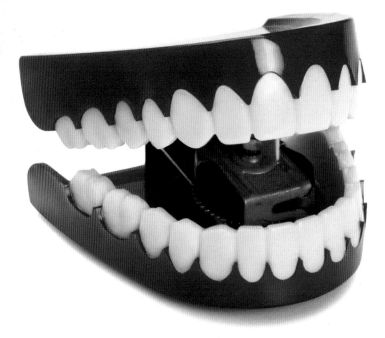

I FIGURE I'LL PEE AND SMOKE A CIG AT THE SAME TIME TO MINIMIZE THE AMOUNT OF TIMES I HAVE TO GET OFF THE COUCH.

Is a bidet an object?

I think so.

I had miles
of more pot
at home,
though.

Your hair is so soft . . . I could sleep in your hair.

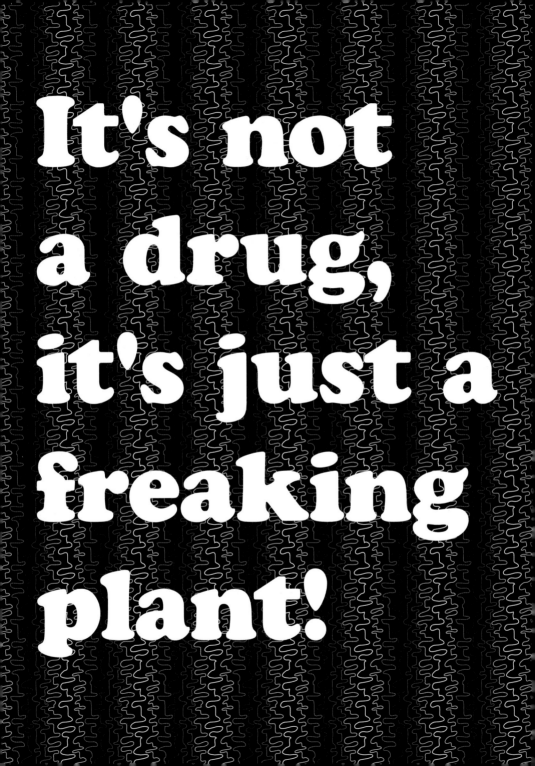

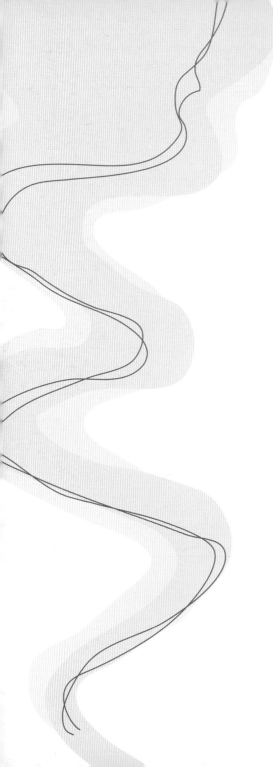

life

Finally, we have come to the biggest pieces of truth, the real philosophical home runs. This section will provide you with the stoner's take on everything, from the implications of astrophysics to Brad Pitt's scuzzy beard.

If you are still bothered by the problems of existence and meaning after you read this section, then I don't think there is any hope for you. Maybe actual, psychiatric help? Or perhaps a book on Cartesian dualism? Just don't get suckered in by *The Secret*.

A lot of the gathered quotes in this section are interrogative, and that is no accident. If you don't find the questions themselves inspirational, then consider the spirit in which they were originally asked. You don't have to accept how things are just because they were told to you. Keep asking and you will find the truth; horrible, raw, and devastating truth.

Let the philosophical catharses begin…

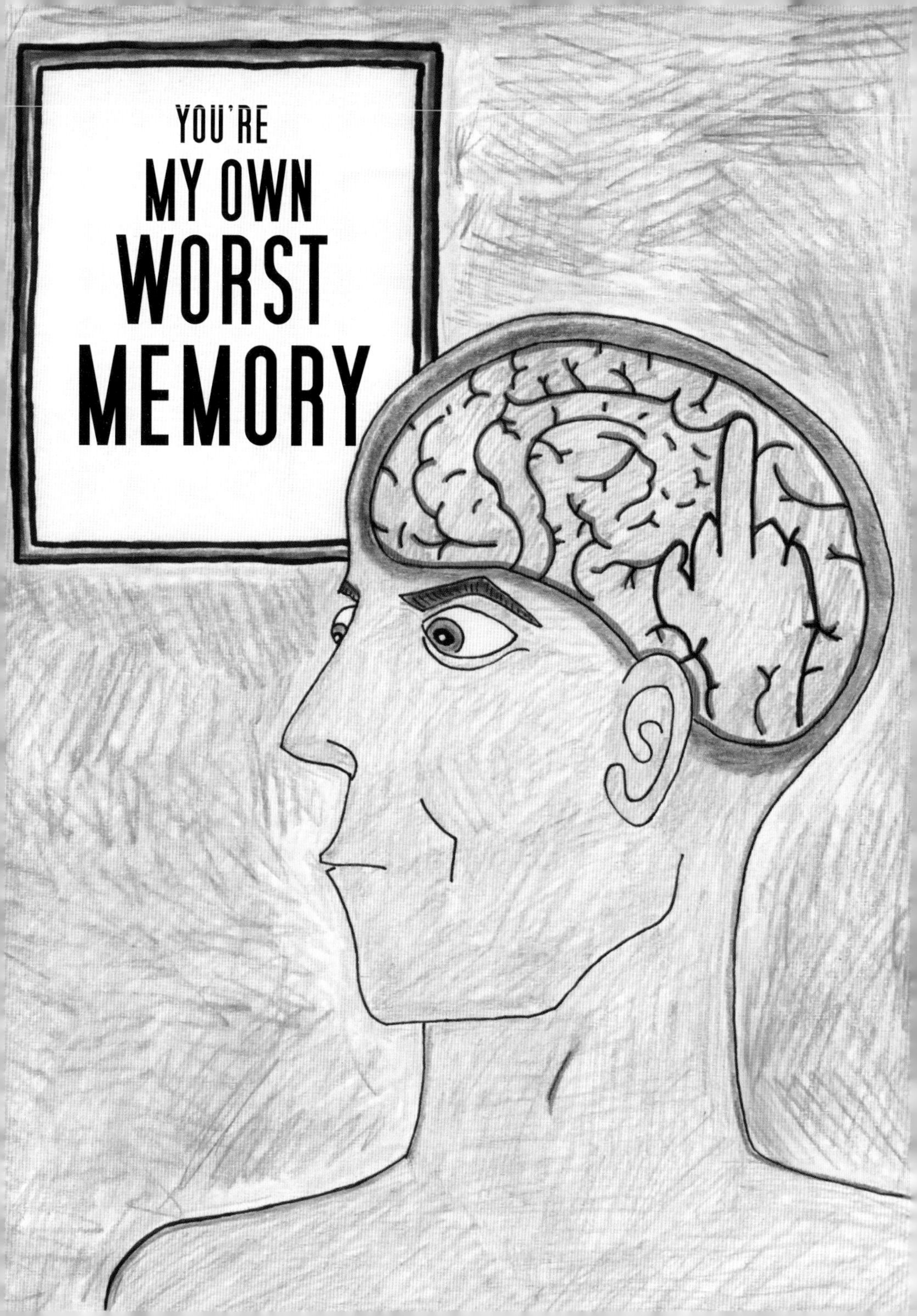
YOU'RE
MY OWN
WORST
MEMORY

Hearing that a star
was really just light
from a million miles
away just blew my
mind as a kid.

Or is it a million years ago?

Now I can't
even remember.

Shouldn't I know that?

IF TIME IS LINEAR ARE WE LINEAR TOO!

Do you think this pot is
laced with anything?

No. Why?

If Hitler lived...

and went to jail...

and then became a
really nice guy...

who never killed
anyone again...,

could you fall in love
with him?

Also, he's like Brad Pitt hot plus the mustache.

Why do people have?
FOREHEADS?
what good do they do?

Man, I bet I look really fuckin' cool right now.

JOHN MAYER
LOOKS LiKE a
STONED MEXICAN.

I JUST REALIZED TODAY I AM THE ONLY I HAVE EVER BEEN

You know no
one's trying to
kill you, right?

Well, they are.

You are absolutely unique.*

*Just like everyone else.

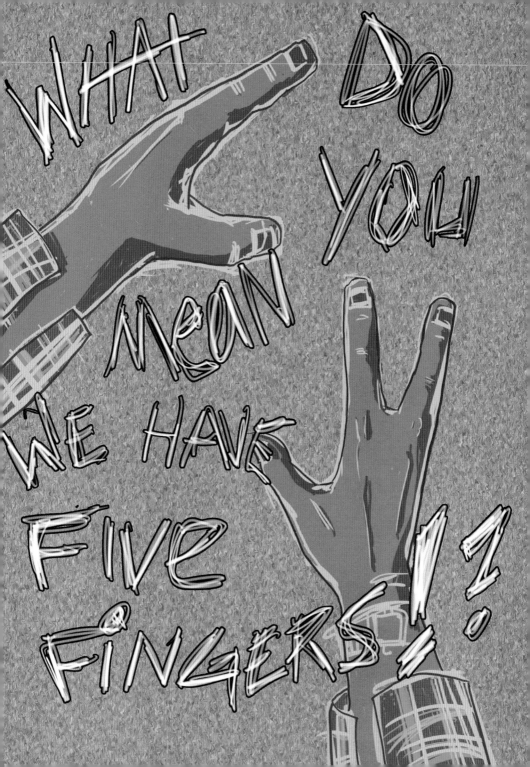

Have you ever noticed that it takes a million times longer to get anywhere when you're stoned but it doesn't really matter?

You're from Montana?
That must be the tingliest of cool.

I DON'T GET HOW TO MEASURE THE SPEED OF LIGHT. IS IT LIKE YOU SET THE TIMER JUST AS YOU FLIP THE SWITCH?

I am going to the place for crazy people
to get the medicine for people who are nuts.

"Oh my god, I love Direct Deposit."
"That has to be the most boring sentence on earth."

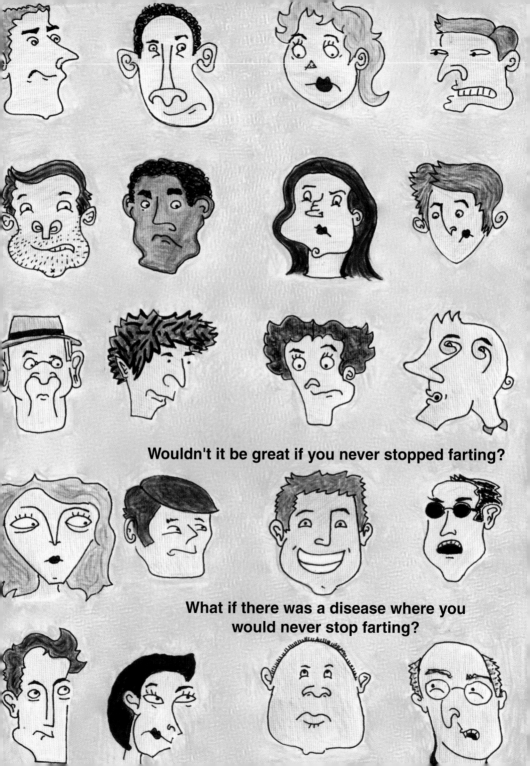

Wouldn't it be great if you never stopped farting?

What if there was a disease where you would never stop farting?

I wonder why my dog chews little Lego guys?

Their legs are the same size as her teeth.

Can't be pleasant.

I think people would be happier if mirrors didn't exist.

Sorry, I was looking at
the flowers on the bag
and got distracted
and forgot the truth.

WHEN YOU SET YOURSELF TO SAYING YOU'RE GOING TO DO SOMETHING, **YOU SHOULD DO IT.** SO WHEN YOU GET DONE YOU CAN SAY THAT YOU CAME TO DO WHAT YOU SAID, **AND YOU DID IT.**

WHERE ARE WE?

I CAN'T FEEL THE AIR.

THERE'S NO GRAVITY.

ARE WE IN SPACE?

I can feel energy
flowing through
the assemblage
point in the small
of my back.

That Carlos Castenda
book was real.

Physics is just like normal, regular math but like

WAAAAY
BIGGER
AMOUNTS!

I can only find ONE SOCK but I guess that's okay. It's not that cold outside.

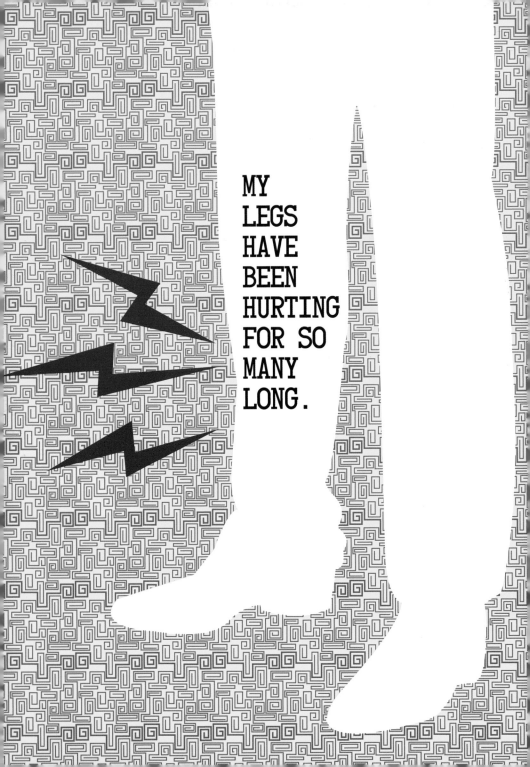

WHITE
PEOPLE
LIKE...

WHAT
WHITE
PEOPLE
LIKE.

You know people say when you marry someone that you're marrying their family too. Why do they call you a daughter- or son-in-law then? Cause who would want to marry their kid? Marriage is gross.

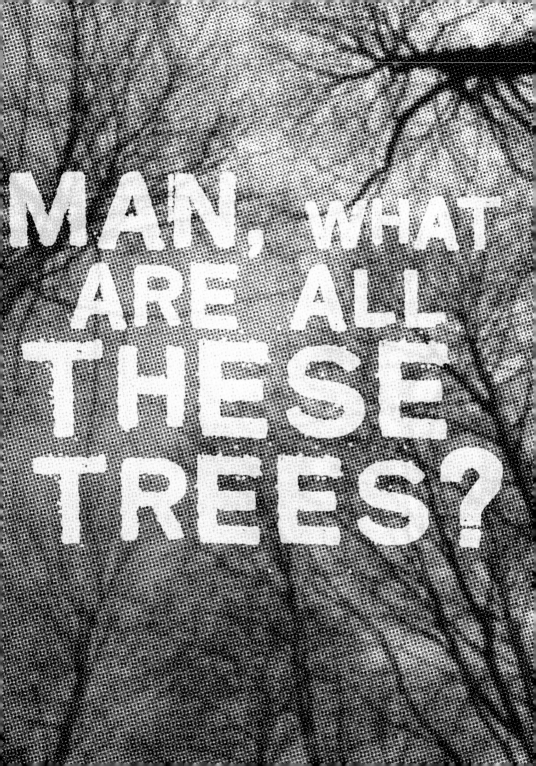

MY EYES FEEL NEW, LIKE I JUST GOT THEM TODAY.

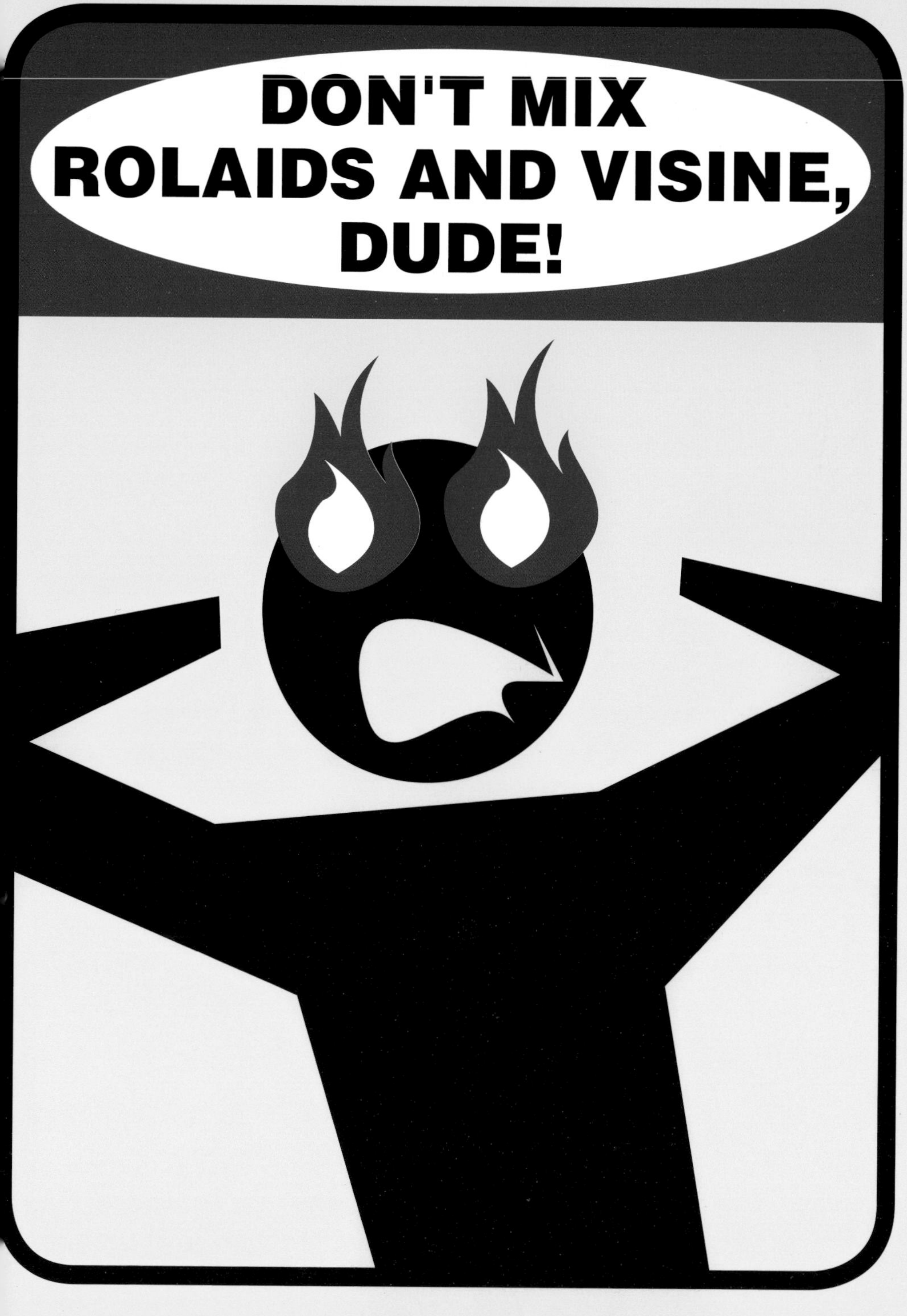
DON'T MIX
ROLAIDS AND VISINE,
DUDE!

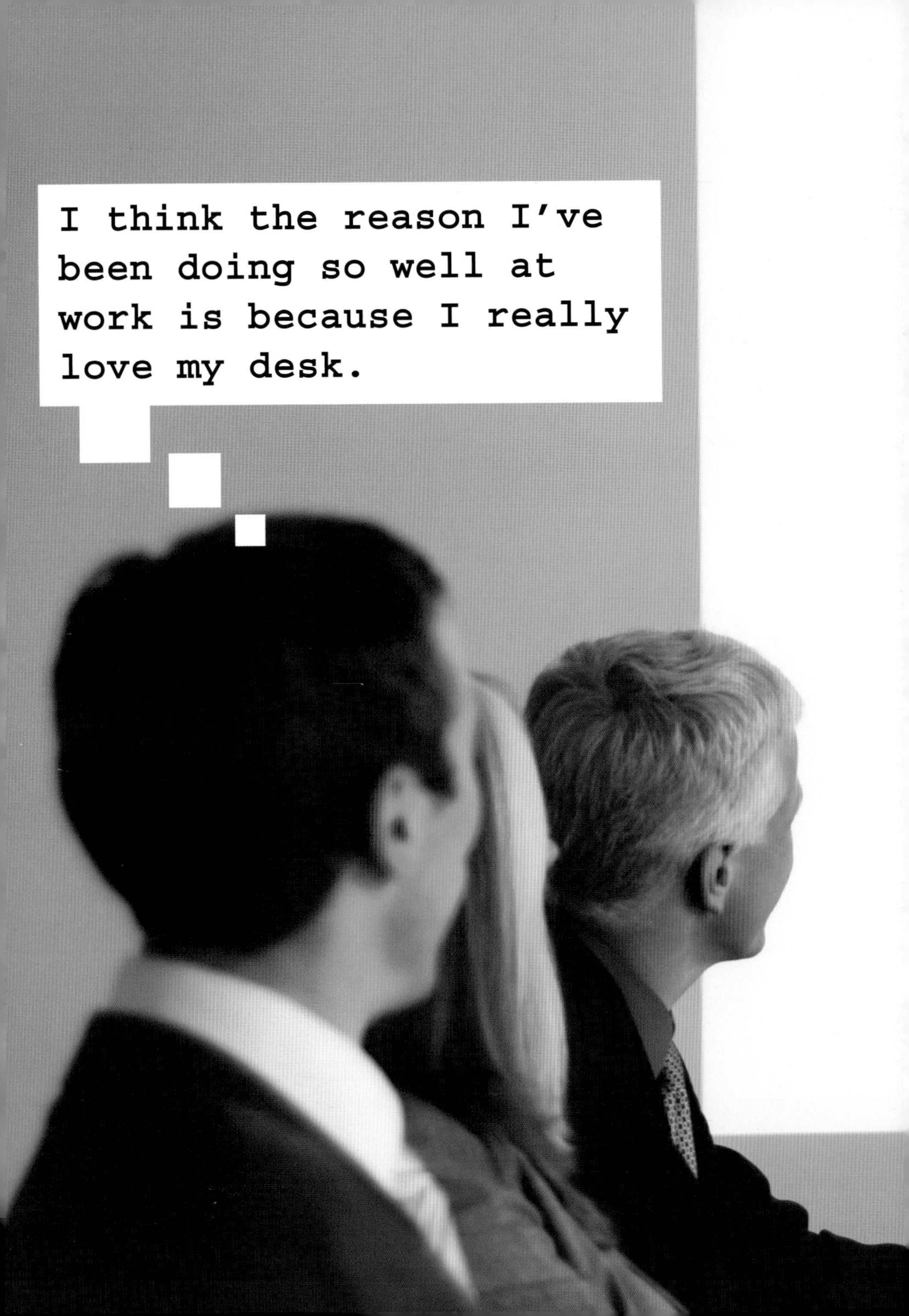
I think the reason I've been doing so well at work is because I really love my desk.

I'M REALLY NOT SURE IF THAT IS A PELICAN OR A PIGEON.

IS IT A
FIVE-FINGERED
DISCOUNT IF
YOU'RE WEARING
MITTENS?

HEY, LET'S MAKE A BOOK THAT LISTS THE DEFINITIONS OF ALL THE WORDS.

IT WOULD BE A BESTSELLER.

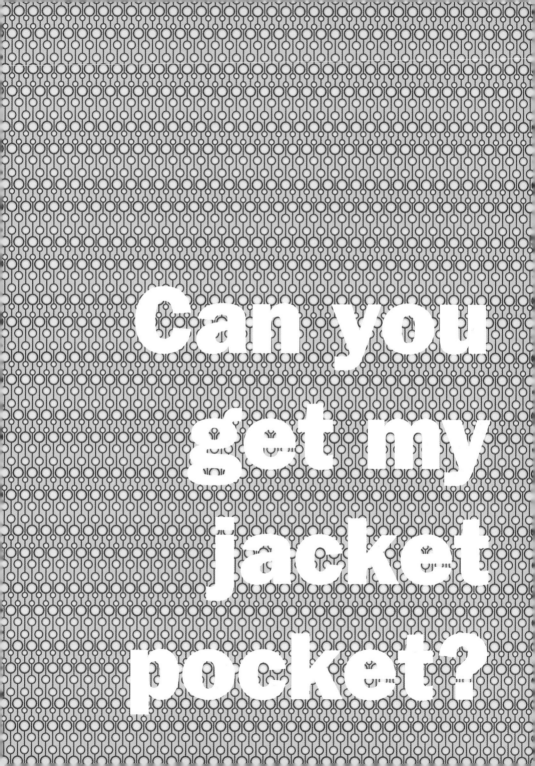

Can you get my jacket pocket?

It feels
like my
heart's in
my eyes.

Is there a
bridge you
can take to
Puerto Rico
from Miami?

Stwitter: Stoned on Twitter. Say it three times fast. Sounds like a stutter.

I got swimmer's ear in both my eyes.

So...

nothing matters?

Adam Bozarth
adambozarthdesign.com

Steve Elmore
stevenelmoreportfolio.com

Will Storie
willstorie.tumblr.com

Matt Mayer
mammothlab.com

the artists

acknowledgments

Thank you first and foremost to the amazing talents of the artists who contributed to this book. I would implore all rich people reading this to go hire them to make beautiful things and pay them obscene amounts of money. It is the dream of every artist, and you can make it come true.

Very special thanks to Tony Lyons, Ann Treistman, and Bill Wolfsthal at Skyhorse Publishing for their invaluable experience, knowledge, and help. Everyone on staff is a champion and will always be a champion.

Many thanks to Kathleen Go for her work on *Things Drunk People Say*. A very hilarious book, and a very high standard to meet.

A tremendous thank you to Molly, for sharing the secrets of the notebook with the world.

To all those who contributed to the book, thank you, and don't forget to spread the love you've shown me out onto the world. Share your wisdom, share your love, share yourself.

your quotes

your quotes